Blockchain

*5 Ways Blockchain
Will Benefit Your Business*

Table of Contents

Introduction 1

Chapter 1: What is Blockchain? 2

Chapter 2: The Blockchain and Smart Contracts 8

Chapter 3: Payments and Money Transfer 12

Chapter 4: Blockchain Data Storage and Cloud Computing 19

Chapter 5: Blockchain and Digital Identity 26

Chapter 6: Blockchain and Supply Chain Management 32

Chapter 7: Networking and Internet of Things 40

Conclusion 44

Introduction

Congratulations and thank you for downloading this book and thank you for.

The following chapters will discuss blockchain and how it can benefit your business. Blockchain is the single most crucial technology in the digital world. It has revolutionized the way we accomplish tasks and introduced new ways of conducting business.

For instance, if your business is collecting data from customers, then you need to ensure that the data is secure and accessible only to authorized users. Current centralized systems can easily be compromised. However, it is impossible to access data within a blockchain system without the necessary authority.

Regardless of the business that you are in, you will still be able to make use of blockchain. For instance, if you wish to store your business information, files and all sorts of data, then you need to identify a blockchain-based cloud storage facility. Such facilities are much cheaper and yet they store data more securely and at much lower costs. Basically, there is so much to look forward to with this amazing technology.

There are plenty of books on this subject on the market, so thanks again for choosing this one! Every effort was made to ensure it is full of as much useful information as possible. Please enjoy!

Chapter 1: What is Blockchain?

Defining Blockchain

At its very core, blockchain is a public, permanent, decentralized, digital, and distributed ledger. The ledger contains data which is then publicly shared by all users within the distributed network.

Tech experts summarize blockchain as simply a mathematical structure used to store data in a manner that is almost impossible to alter. You can use the blockchain to store just about any type of data.

Main purpose

The main function of a blockchain is to record transactions and store data. This data is stored in the form of blocks which are regularly added to the network. Therefore, the blockchain is ever growing in size. Blockchain was originally referred to as "block chain." The blocks in the network are joined together using cryptography.

A single block within the blockchain network consists of a timestamp, a cryptograph hash that points to the previous block, and data. It is normally just about impossible to modify any data stored within a block. This makes any data stored in a block irrevocable and the blockchain itself incorruptible.

Distributed Ledger

The blockchain is used as a distributed ledger. In such an instance, all transactions and other operations are managed on a peer-to-peer network. Any person or computer connected to the network is referred to as a node. Whenever data is entered into the system, each node is updated simultaneously. If data is to be altered, removed, changed, or deleted, then the entire network has to be in agreement and the transaction has to be done simultaneously. For large, distributed networks, such a feat is almost impossible to achieve. This is why a distributed system is considered incorruptible.

| centralised | decentralised | distributed |

Blockchain was originally designed and developed to provide an accounting framework for Bitcoin, a virtual currency. However, it now finds use in numerous applications. It is mostly used in commerce, businesses, and industry to accomplish certain objectives.

In the world of cryptocurrencies, the blockchain is used primarily for the verification of transactions and sometimes for the creation of new crypto tokens. However, it is possible to change the code and digitize the blockchain so that it can work for just any other system. These include applications for the banking sector, stock market, corporate accounting solutions, and so much more. All the records within the blockchain are indelible. Because of this, companies are guaranteed to save money and prevent losses that would otherwise occur using other types of systems.

Blockchain is a Distributed Ledger

A distributed ledger consists of a record of all entries and transactions within a system. Every time a transaction occurs, the ledger is updated and all users are notified. The ledger is said to be distributed because all users connected to it are able to access it.

Centralized Systems

There are centralized systems where users gain access to shared information from a single point. For instance, most current systems used by businesses and even banks rely on a centralized server. Under such a system, only one person or entity is in charge of the entire system even there are often numerous other users. Users can suffer loss, lack of service, poor service, fraud, and so on through a centralized system.

There is still a lot of mistrust in such a system. For instance, citizens around the world are unhappy with banks that control who can and who cannot use their systems. This is something that a lot of consumers are unhappy with. They prefer a system that is more secure and trustworthy.

The benefit of using a blockchain is that it does not discriminate against users. Anyone is free to join a blockchain and use the service provided. It is not controlled by one single entity. Instead, it operates using a protocol that is agreeable to everyone. Users are notified any time a transaction takes place or when data is entered into the system. This is a more transparent approach to matters of finance, banking, accounting and so on. Blockchain provides an apt solution to the issue of inclusivity, trust, speed, and reliability.

Blockchain Application

Due to its nature, and the use of a distributed computing system, the blockchain finds application in numerous sectors. These range from the fields of academia and research to medical records, food traceability, land management, financial records, stock market transactions, identity management, voting in democratic elections, and so much more. The possibilities of such a system are virtually endless.

Inherent Possibilities of a Blockchain Network

The world today makes use of intermediaries in numerous ways. For instance, a business pays its workers, suppliers, and shareholders using intermediaries such as banks. Other intermediaries include social media companies, governments, and credit card companies among others.

While these intermediaries perform an important function, they add a layer to the execution of the transaction. This adds costs, slows down the process, and gives too much power to these institutions. Take for instance banks and financial institutions. They get to determine who can open an account and which accounts can be shut down.

Centralized systems are also very prone to attacks, compromise, and hacking. A lot of institutions have fallen prey to hackers, thieves, pranksters, and to other criminal activity that is rather harmful. Such forms of crime cannot be perpetuated on the blockchain because the criminals would have to hack into all the nodes within the network at the same time. Banks exclude people with little or no money from the financial system. Governments and banks have had their central servers hacked into.

In the world of intermediaries, financial services are very slow and costly. Think about a wire transfer that takes 2 to 3 days to execute. For instance, an email takes less than a second from a sender to receiver. The blockchain will reduce both the time and cost of transacting making it a lot faster and much cheaper as well as. Intermediaries make lots of money, slow down transactions, and have a lot of power.

Blockchain—The Distributed, Digital, Network

If the blockchain was to replace the current centralized systems, then it will be easier for businesses to transact and conduct their affairs. It will be possible to move a variety of digital assets ranging from software to music to currency. These assets could be exchanged, stored, moved, and transacted with ease.

Blockchain is widely used in the digital currency services. Cryptocurrencies like Bitcoin and Ethereum all use the blockchain. This means anyone anywhere in the world is able to transact, send money, make purchases, and much more because of the possibilities provided by the blockchain. Think about transferring these opportunities to other spheres or sectors of the economy.

Blockchain is expected to affect numerous sectors and introduce major changes to the way we conduct business, do things, communicate, and interact. It will operate via the Internet of Things. Anyone who uses the blockchain will be able to transact with others through trust and usually without an intermediary. Any assets or information transacted across a network are distributed to each user or each node. Transactions will be instantly processed and costs will come down drastically.

Blockchain uses cryptography which is a technique used to encrypt data so that it cannot be breached. This technique uses complex mathematics and principles of computer science in order to protect data in the presence of a third party. Cryptography is really all about constructing and setting up protocols that prevent third parties from accessing private data.

Challenges of Centralized Systems

There exist a lot of challenges with the current centralized systems. Centralized systems such as those used by banks, other financial institutions and even governments have spurned mistrust and concern over the years. Some of the activities of some banks have been highly unethical and a few have bordered on illegal. Lots of Americans, and possibly people elsewhere around the world, have shown very little confidence in current banks and other financial institutions.

There is a definite need to change the current centralized system and adopt a more trustworthy system that is not just credible and reliable but also one that instills confidence in the public. This is why there is excitement about the blockchain, its properties, and its application in major industries. The blockchain is a distributed network that ensures the security of a system, transparency, and speed. Such systems do not rely on a centralized server or system.

Blockchain is expected to have a profound impact on our lives in the coming years. Apart from being the backbone of most cryptocurrencies, it is expected to power the next generation internet. Blockchain holds huge promise from most industries, individuals, and sectors of the economy.

The Internet of Value

The current internet in use today is known as the internet of information. We use for purposes of sharing data, exchanging photos and videos, sending emails and similar things. Even then, whenever we send something, we are really actually sending a copy. If we send a document, we are usually left with the original. The recipient receives a copy. What if a bank was to send money via the internet? It would still retain the same amount in its accounts. This can be a rather worrying trend. If we are to send or exchange things of value, where no copies are allowed, then we should have a better system.

A new type of internet is necessary. It is known as the "Internet of Value". By using this type of internet, we can send things of value such as currency, land titles, certificates, motor vehicle registration and so on. Such a network can also be used to transact intellectual property and even carbon credits. And the best part is that there will be no need for intermediaries like banks. For instance, if a person needs credit and another is willing to advance a loan, they can negotiate terms on the blockchain and transact without an intermediary. This cuts costs and helps save time.

Advanced blockchains such as Blockchain 2.0 like the one used by Ethereum are a little more advanced compared to Blockchain 1.0 widely used on the Bitcoin platform. It can run smart contracts which are essentially contracts that self-execute. Such contracts can be designed and then executed to achieve certain extremely useful purposes.

With proper management and administration, the blockchain can manage elections and support transactions at the financial markets. According to tech insiders, the first internet—the internet of information—brought a lot of wealth but did not spread it around. It is hoped that the Internet of Things will help spread the wealth so there is shared prosperity and reduced social inequality.

Chapter 2: The Blockchain and Smart Contracts

An Introduction to Smart Contracts

Smart contracts can be defined as a computer program or protocol that is designed to enforce, facilitate, or verify the performance and execution of a contract.

A smart contract enables the execution of all sorts of digital contracts without the need for a third party. The best part of these contracts is that all transactions are irreversible and each stage can be tracked. Many different types of clauses with a smart contract can be made fully or partially self-enforcing, self-executing, or even both.

Such contracts are necessary because the nature of security they provide is much higher than conventional contract law. They also help reduce other costs that may be associated with the contract. There are a number of cryptocurrencies such as Ethereum that have adopted and run smart contracts.

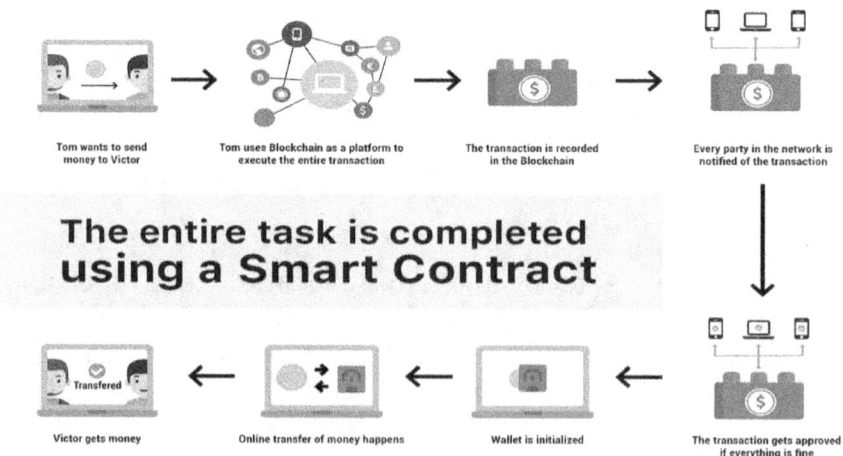

Tom wants to send money to Victor

Tom uses Blockchain as a platform to execute the entire transaction

The transaction is recorded in the Blockchain

Every party in the network is notified of the transaction

The entire task is completed using a Smart Contract

Victor gets money

Online transfer of money happens

Wallet is initialized

The transaction gets approved if everything is fine

Smart Contracts and Businesses

Smart contracts have now become essential for businesses. If you own a business and wish to cut on costs and improve performance, then you should find out how you can integrate your current information and communications infrastructure with smart contracts that are essential for your business.

In recent years, there has been an increased demand for blockchain programmers. Sadly, they are in short supply. Business owners should consider training their own in-house programmers. Small businesses may want to consult a software and programming firm to have their own smart contracts developed.

Ordinary businesses will consider this as a cost. However, it is better if this is viewed as an investment because the benefits and returns will be immense over the years. Smart contracts and the blockchain promise higher returns, productivity, and increased opportunities in the future.

Origin of Smart Contracts

A young computer scientist known as Nick Szabo came up with the term smart contracts. He wanted these to be executed and run on the blockchain. According to a recent report by the US government, the concept of smart contracts is largely based on basic contract law. With such contracts, unlike traditional ones, a computer program will enforce the contract which is ordinarily built into the computer code.

Smart contracts are designed to enforce and verify contracts by using various cryptographic protocols as well as additional digital security mechanisms.

While smart contracts are able to replace certain aspects of normal contracts, they are, in an actual sense, not entirely a legal concept. They tend to offer a technical solution in support of business transactions. This kind of approach helps propel businesses to profitability. You can think of smart contracts as computer code that is developed by a blockchain expert and inserted into a distributed network. They help to simplify a lot of the processes that should be accomplished and verified by you or your workers. This makes your office computer network a totally reliable auditor.

Businesses and Smart Contracts

Smart contracts apply to all sorts of businesses. They have been proven to be especially effective in supply chain management operations. Every person within the supply chain on a decentralized blockchain gains access and insights into the recorded data and transactions. Active participants are also able to keep track of all incidents and occurrences at all points regarding both location and time.

If your company or business is considering using smart contract services, all you need to do is have a developer come up with a contract or protocols that can validate multiple transactions. However, the transactions should not just include values or entries. It should include additional specifications such as quantities, qualities, and other essential ones that are essential for the validity of the transaction. The planned or agreed event should only take place once all the set conditions are met and within the agreed timeframe.

Instructions within a smart contract can be adjusted or changed if both parties to the contract are in agreement. If parties are not in agreement then the instructions are impossible to change. A good example is a contract where all group members need to append their signatures. Without all the signatures available, the second stage of the contract cannot be executed.

Smart contracts offer businesses a whole new level of protection from any unknown outcomes. The records and data within the contract occur in a distributed ledger which means they are permanent, irrevocable, traceable, and immutable. Some of the most important aspects of smart contracts are consensus, permanency, and immutability.

These protect all participants from any untoward behavior or activity from others. While they may not necessarily be perfect due to a possible human error during execution, they offer a much higher level of protection, help cut costs, and improve on the time it takes to perform certain tasks. Some examples where smart contracts come in handy in business include verification of data, prevention of multiple transactions, digital payments, and a lot more.

Chapter 3: Payments and Money Transfer

Businesses like yours are always making and receiving payments. You need to pay your suppliers, pay taxes, meet the costs of overheads and also pay your workers. On the other hand, you receive payments from customers and clients for the products and services that you provide.

Traditional payment methods have worked just fine. However, they are perceived to be slow, tedious, and expensive especially in the face of new technologies. It is now possible, using the blockchain technology, to send and receive money to almost anyone instantly. You will soon be able to send large amounts of money in almost an instant and at a very low cost to you.

Challenges with Cross-border Cash Transfers

Funds transfer, cash remittance, and overseas payments are transactions that involve moving cash from an account in one country to an account or person in another.

Across borders, financial institutions use the services of SWIFT. It handles messages moved with payments across borders. It is the corresponding banking institutions that actually perform the credits and debits across accounts depending on messages received. SWIFT also ensures that the value being transmitted is actually forwarded to recipients.

First, the banks will charge senders a fee in order to process each and every transaction. This has the effect of adding a cost to the cash transmission. Messages are posted onto SWIFT and fees are charged for this. The purpose of SWIFT during finds transmission is to ensure that any debit entry in a bank's ledger is concisely communicated to the relevant bank in order to pass the corresponding credit entry in an accurate fashion as required.

SWIFT guarantees and confirms transmission of messages because banks cannot agree on transactions according to their own ledgers. It then charges both sending and receiving banks while Central banks are used as settlement agents in order to guarantee payments. There is a series of corresponding banks that deal with matters such as netting payment messages, collating, and receiving messages before transmission. This tends to increase the time it takes to process payments.

Central banks around the world often insist that banks should have sufficient liquidity in their central bank settlements account to help process any such transfers or payments.

Digital Cash Platforms

At the moment there are numerous firms providing financial services on digital money platforms. These have been proven to work efficiently and are effective for business purposes. The only drawback is that the processes are not yet the standard but this is only a matter of time. Within a few years' time, almost all businesses will move the bulk of their payments to blockchain-backed platforms.

There are numerous challenges encountered by both businesses and individuals when sending money overseas or even making payments. First, money is lost when converting one currency into another. Also, there are fees and costs as well as time taken to remit money. According to a study, it costs between 7% and 10% in fees of the total money transferred. This is really costly especially when huge amounts are being sent.

Using blockchain, the fees and charges reduce drastically. The World Bank has, for instance, noted that a reduction in transaction fees can help save huge amounts. Just a 5% reduction, for example, can help save businesses billions of dollars. Blockchain technology provides a firm foundation for the fast, affordable, and reliable financial transactions.

Using blockchain, transactions are encrypted then entered into a ledger so that all relevant members of a blockchain network have access to the ledger entries. Such transactions cannot be altered and so blockchain is considered as impervious to fraud. Blockchain is a peer-to-peer network which means any single user can interact and transact directly with each other without the need for a third party such as a bank.

Challenges of Traditional Money Transmission Methods

Regular commercial and even investment banks are unable to send money directly to a client. This is because no two banks can process a transaction and agree based on their own ledgers. They have to use a third party, SWIFT. SWIFT will process transactions between banks and charge both institutions fees. There is also a need to interact with numerous corresponding banks to enable a transaction. All these processes slow down transactions and increase costs of cash transfer.

Solutions to the Problem of Effective Cash Transfer

We have seen that the blockchain can provide a suitable alternative when it comes to cash transfers, especially international transfers. All that is needed is a peer-to-peer network. If two businesses operate on such a network, then they can interact, agree on terms and transfer cash between them at very low costs. The transfers between two entities or nodes within a network cost almost nothing. The transactions also occur almost seamlessly.

Transactions on a blockchain are verified by the block and cannot be altered or reversed. All members of the network will receive an update of any such transaction so there will be a permanent record. Also, since there are no intermediaries and no corresponding banks to deal with, transactions occur instantly.

There will be a need to use tokens, however. Blockchains use digital currencies for transactions and transfers. Once the transfer is sent digitally to your account, you will then only need to decide how you wish to deal with your payment in its digital form.

How Cash Transfer and Digital Payments Work

Let's say you want to pay Zach in Canada. You will log into your blockchain-based account and enter the details of your transactions into a block. These details will be shared among all members of the network. The network has a team of miners or validators. They will receive the details of the transaction and then process them instantly. Once approved, the blockchain is updated and the transaction proceeds. These records become public, indelible, permanent, and irreversible. Zach in Canada will receive his money in minutes at a very low cost.

Critical Aspects of Blockchain Adoption and Money Transfer

There is still plenty of ongoing research all around the world by banks and major financial institutions to perform proof-of-concept and other much-needed research. Firms that provided funds transfer services are often referred to as FinTech companies. They are not banks but often provide the necessary facilitation needed to make payments and send money to others within a network.

Other factors being worked out include the need for data protection and privacy. It is crucial that users do not have their data or personal information compromised in any way. Also of great importance is compliance with the law and abiding by regulations. Financial institutions understand the importance of adhering to regulations and compliance at all times. While there are no current regulations managing blockchain transactions, it is good to keep up with developments in this field.

The Benefits of Using Blockchain Financial Transactions

- The use of blockchain largely gets rid of middlemen and intermediaries. It also eliminates centralized entities like banks and regulators. Most of the time these tend to make the entire process tedious which is undesirable especially in a business environment.

- No one is excluded from transactions. The blockchain platform allows any individual and any entity to open an account and transact. Traditional payment methods like use of banks and similar institutions operate differently. They can deny some users access to their platforms.

- There is a drastic reduction in fees, costs, and charges. Charges that are eliminated during international cash transfer and payments include SWIFT charges and corresponding bank charges and any other third parties involved.

- You will notice much lower turnaround time for all transactions and settlements. This is because intermediaries, central banks, and clearance houses are not a part of the equation. Banks also need to ensure there is intraday liquidity in order to process transactions. This requirement is eliminated on the blockchain.

- The blockchain operates differently as balances are verified during transactions. Balances are usually known and determined because they are maintained within the same system where transactions will be conducted.

- Also, transaction details are both hashed and encrypted. The transactions are visible to both parties at the same time so there is increased transparency. This compares favorably to banks whose operations are shrouded in secrecy and it is almost impossible to learn about certain crucial details pertaining to transactions.

There are a couple of challenges in regards to privacy and data protection. Experts, however, believe that these are challenges that could be addressed. For instance, businesses can opt for blockchains where not everyone can join and gain access to private information. This will mean signing up to agreements for bilateral engagements. Parties can use access keys to access specific data that pertains to their operations. This ensures that privacy is maintained even as the integrity of the blockchain and transaction are upheld. There is also a level of difficulty in hacking the system to make changes. The cryptography used as well as blockchain technology make hacking or unauthorized use almost impossible.

New Systems and Testing Underway

There are a number of organizations, mostly in the tech and finance industries, conducting experiments on the use of distributed ledgers for the transfer of money and payments between individuals and businesses. The most popular platform in use at the moment is the blockchain used by Ethereum. This blockchain is regarded as Blockchain 2.0.

Blockchain 2.0 is a lot more advanced compared to Blockchain 1.0, the one used by Bitcoin. There are a couple of differences why one is better than the other. Let us examine blockchain 2.0 closely.

Blockchain 2.0

The blockchain which Ethereum runs is known as blockchain 2.0. It was developed by a Canadian computer scientist by the name Vitalik Buterin. This blockchain has some advanced features and is superior compared to the original blockchain such as the one used by bitcoin.

It is on blockchain 2.0 where smart contracts can be executed. Smart contracts can help accomplish a lot and replace a lot of current systems. Even financial transactions can be executed on the blockchain 2.0. In the world of finances, most of the processes are tedious and time-consuming. Such processes can be reduced to smart contracts that have the capacity to self-execute. This cuts the time it takes to execute financial processes and also helps to curb costs.

Regulatory Reporting by Leveraging Big Data

Blockchain provides high levels of security to users. However, there is a need for statutory or regulatory reporting, especially if the institutions involved are banks. Regulators require banks to report transactions, including payments and remittances from overseas.

In such situations, then an additional data layer is necessary within the blockchain. This data layer should be integrated into the payment process. The registered details provided to the banks via the nodes within the network. This kind of set-up works best in permission enabled blockchain where only users with the necessary permission and protocols can access certain services or view certain information. Now data from the entire network is captured into a big data setup. At this stage, the data will be in the form of hashes. It will need to be converted into a regular format and aligned with the data held by banks. When this happens, then reporting will be easier and the regulators can receive the essential or statutory reports with all the required details.

Chapter 4: Blockchain Data Storage and Cloud Computing

By now we have established that the blockchain and all affiliated applications are the future of technology. We have seen that financial transactions and smart contracts can be effortlessly executed on the blockchain. The blockchain provides a faster, less costly, and more efficient way of doing things. The same applies to cloud storage.

Speed is crucial in today's workplace. Business owners, corporations, individuals, and all consumers need fast and seamless access to information. According to a study conducted in 2009, most cloud users expected a page to load or download a page in 2 seconds or less. Basically, pages that did not load in 3 seconds were abandoned by 40% of users. This study is almost 10 years old which means expectations are even higher today.

Customers are not likely to sit around and wait for information to load. They expect pages to load within minimal time. Video buffering and image loading need not take time but should happen instantly. Today, search engines like Google also use a website's speed as part of its ranking criteria. This is why more and more businesses are using networks such as CDNS, content distribution, and delivery networks, to help improve speed. Blockchain technology promises to introduce the high speeds that customers, clients, users expect. Fortunately, the trend today is headed towards blockchain and similar technologies.

How Traditional Cloud Services Work

Think about subscribing to Google Drive service in order to store your personal data. Google Drive is a cloud storage service available to members. Traditional storage services were centralized with companies and organizations having their own servers at the office or elsewhere.

While centralized server data storage allows companies a lot of control, costs are high because of the need for in-house computer experts as well as external backup services to provide redundancy. Cloud services have become extremely popular across the globe. Firms such as Google, Amazon, Dropbox and numerous others have flourished in this area.

Challenges

There are a number of challenges that come with the use of giant server farms. First of all, operating them daily is costly. There are things such as temperature control, rigorous maintenance, updates, and a lot more. A lot of parts need to be replaced on a regular basis. Also, large data centers that host huge computer storage servers do affect the environment in a big way. Another factor that comes into play is the issue of safety. There is always the risk that things could go wrong and this poses an additional risk. Traditional cloud storage poses risk and dangers of a security breach and unauthorized access.

This is where traditional cloud storage facilities come in handy. Firms like Amazon and Google offer storage services to companies. Cloud storage allows companies to store large amounts of data at offsite locations. This data is backed up several times and can be accessed from any location at any time of day or night. The service providers charge a small monthly or annual fee.

For instance, Amazon S3 charges about $25 per terabyte of data each month. This is incredible value for money and is much cheaper for companies compared to managing their own storage facilities. The data is stored in multiple locations and this ensures that it is always available and cannot be compromised no matter what.

However, with all these benefits comes the risk or issue relating to trust. There is too much trust bestowed on the cloud service providers. Consider the amount of data that a company stores within a cloud. The company will have to trust the service provider with useful and important files. These third parties are trusted to secure very private and highly sensitive information. The data on cloud storage is usually not encrypted.

Also, while your data is safe, it can always be legally accessed and the data shared with others. This fact can be found in the privacy terms where different scenarios play out. And while the cost of storage may seem low, there is really no suitable point of reference. A lot of experts draw parallels between the centralized cloud storage system and current financial systems. They rely on third parties for a lot of functions. Fortunately, they can all easily be replaced by a blockchain-based cloud storage.

Blockchain-Based Cloud Computing and Data Storage

It is possible to create blockchain-based cloud storage that offers distributed, decentralized, and secure cloud storage marketplace. We are all aware of the kind of excitement that the blockchain has brought. It holds huge promise especially in the world of finance.

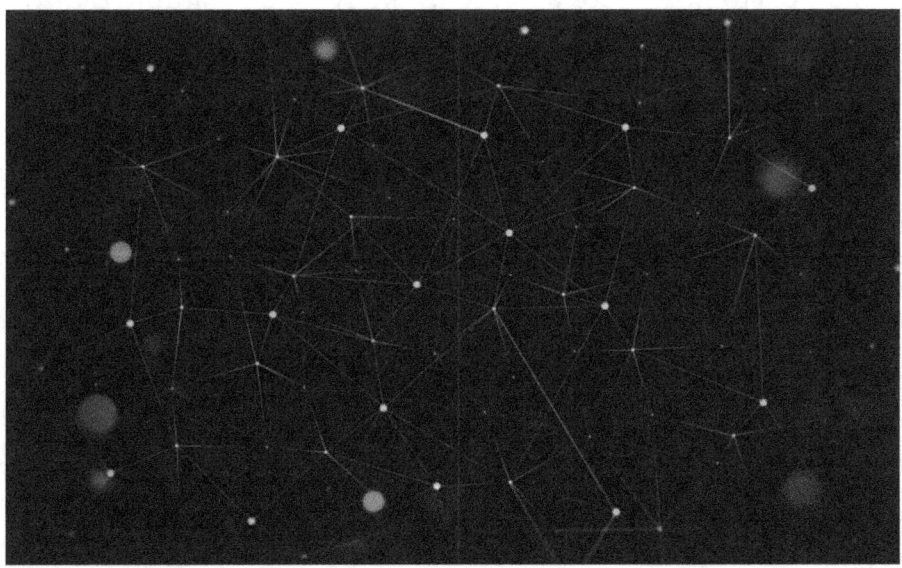

Blockchain-based cloud storage

When it comes to cloud storage, blockchain offers excellent solutions. Storage infrastructure has changed a lot for the last couple of years. There is a shift now from centralized systems to more distributed, public cloud storage systems. Companies do so in order to reduce and avoid costs and functions related to in-house storage challenges. It also allows them access to certain features and resources that they need. This is why there has been such massive growth in the cloud computing industry.

The challenges with current centralized cloud computing systems are not farfetched. Service interruptions and data breaches, for instance, are not uncommon. In 2017, the main concern that businesses and individuals had with cloud storage had to do with data breaches. Identity theft, theft of industry secrets, hacking and all manner of vices are rampant. The weakness of such system lies in their centralized nature.

Take for instance the instance where up to 6 million records were tampered with. Verizon is one of America's largest communication companies. Unfortunately, its data stored with Amazon S3 cloud storage service was violated. Records of over 6 million customers were accessed. The reason is simply that the storage server used by Amazon was neither secure nor protected.

There was another breach when another US firm, Deep Roots Analytics, misconfigured its servers. Due to the misconfiguration, the servers were violated and sensitive customer details, about 198 million records, were accessed without authorization. Experts say that these are not isolated cases but examples of what happens from time to time due to the use of centralized storage systems.

Fortunately, blockchains are able to address the issue of unauthorized access. By their very nature, they are almost impossible to hack. Also, the information used is protected using cryptography. This adds another layer of protection making it almost impossible to breach information within a blockchain network.

If you are storing your company's information on a cloud then you are placing immense trust in a third party. This can be pretty risky if you are storing sensitive information. This is why there is a shift from centralized cloud computing and storage systems to distributed, decentralized systems. While the centralized system has numerous benefits, the blockchain benefits are far too great to ignore.

Blockchain Technology for Cloud Storage

When it comes to cloud storage and computing, much of the work will still be managed centrally but then controlled using a blockchain approach. Therefore, even if the data is distributed throughout a network, the workload will be executed centrally. In essence, the blockchain manages to create a distributed and decentralized data storage marketplace.

The blockchain technology used for data storage and cloud computing can be rather technical because of the complex data structure used. There are lots of companies including startups that are currently utilizing blockchain storage platforms. These platforms are also referred to as marketplaces because the host sells storage space and cloud services. Customers pay for space where they store their files and data in various forms.

Payments for cloud services are often made within the blockchain. Files received are first broken down and fragmented after initial encryption. They are then smartly distributed across different nodes in different countries around the world. There are dozens of such nodes all over the globe. This secures data and makes it just about impossible to breach. Data remains safe and cannot be stolen or accessed without authorization.

Why Blockchain Cloud Computing is Preferred

Take the case of Amazon S3 cloud storage service. Here, data in the form of files is stored among different computers spread out across the globe. While this helps to accomplish redundancy, it still leaves points of weaknesses as each individual computer server is liable to hacking. With the blockchain, however, all the data is completely decentralized as it is stored across multiple nodes spread out globally. Users get a lot more protection especially when it comes to errors that may occur during transmitting or storing data.

The blockchain introduces privacy which is a challenge that centralized servers in traditional cloud computing have been unable to hack. Users, including businesses and individuals, get to enjoy a lot more privacy because user files and data are not managed and controlled fully by a single entity. What happens is that files are broken up and encrypted. Then encrypted fragments are stored across multiple computers, or nodes, using keys that each user receives.

This is a great approach to privacy and data security because other users with access to the nodes will not be able to access your files and data. The encryption is such that the data can only be viewed using the key which you are issued with. And if by the remotest chance a host node managed to access your file, it is only a partial file which will mean absolutely nothing to them. This shows that it is almost impossible to compromise any store data within the blockchain cloud.

However, the most crucial factor for most business owners and users is lower cost. For instance, Amazon S3 charges about $25 per terabyte for one month while the same service costs only $2 per month. This provides significant savings, which is great for small business owners. There are a couple of cloud data storage facilities out there using the blockchain. They include StorJ, File Coin, and Maid Safe among others. A lot of these are the preferred option for businesses and other organizations because of better security, faster uptime, and lower costs.

Each of these platforms leases out unused hard drive storage space within their nodes spread out around the world. The cloud storage companies need users to make use of free space on their hard drives. Even though prices are arbitrary, large service providers actually make impressive profits from leasing out cloud storage space. In most cases, demand for the remote storage and cloud computing services will vary throughout the year.

Blockchain cloud services make use of already existing servers and networks so the cost of setting them up is not as high as might be thought. If you do not believe in cryptocurrencies such as bitcoin and all the others, you can at least believe that blockchain technology is here to stay. Blockchain is strongly believed to be the technology of the twenty-first century given its properties and low costs.

Advantages of Decentralized Cloud Services

1. Decentralized data storage provides additional privacy and security. Such systems are much more difficult to hack compared to traditional, centralized, servers. On decentralized systems, files are split into several segments and spread out across various nodes. This process is known as sharding.

2. There are some blockchains that allow the use of cryptocurrencies. Anyone interested in selling storage simply needs to buy space on the platforms and lease it out to any interested person or business entity. Basically, there is a ready market created.

3. It is almost impossible to lose files on the blockchain cloud. This is because there are copies of the original data files stored across different nodes. It is possible for errors to occur during transmission but total loss of data or files is absolutely not possible.

4. The prices have reduced drastically and almost any individual or business owner can afford to lease storage space on the blockchain.

Decentralized storage facilities can be beneficial to both business owners and individuals as they protect information and secure data at much lower costs. There are companies offering these services at affordable costs. Blockchain technology will cause serious disruption to the cloud computing and storage service. Just about anyone, including institutions, organizations, and corporations will benefit from the affordable storage services.

Due to costs, security, speed, and other factors, blockchain storage marketplaces have the potential to replace the large centralized systems provided by Microsoft, Google, Amazon, Dropbox, and others.

Chapter 5: Blockchain and Digital Identity

Technology experts have railed blockchain as the biggest technology invention of the twenty-first century. It is said to be the most crucial invention since the advent of the internet. It is now poised to change completely the way we do business. One of the most serious crimes today is identity theft. Consumers across the globe are afraid of their personal information falling into the wrong hands. Unfortunately, this tends to occur all too often.

Blockchain and Digital Identity

As the world becomes more and more digitized, the importance of personal identity also increases. Fortunately, blockchain technology is here with us. It provides the necessary technology that we need in order to ensure that we can securely store personal information.

With blockchain, we are able to trust in applications that deal with digital identity. These not only enable the storage of our personal information but also enable us to transfer assets using our digital identities. Asset transfer is going to go digital where soft assets like currencies and hard assets like land and property can be digitally transferred from one person to another.

Current Systems

We transact online on a regular basis and leave a digital footprint everywhere we go. Basically, the more websites we visit the larger the digital traces that gets left behind. Take financial processing websites. There are plenty of these and they include major platforms like PayPal, Google Wallet, Amazon Pay, Apple Pay, and numerous others. They also include cryptocurrency platforms, online banking, and credit card processors. On all these sites, we need to leave our identities. Personal and financial information is necessary in order to transact on all these platforms.

Currently, personal data is stored in different databases and then generated on varying occasions depending on the need. Sometimes our addresses or phone numbers change but this does not reflect on all these databases. This results in multiple digital identities across all the various databases online.

It is quite obvious that there are numerous challenges with the current systems of digital identity systems. One of these challenges is that users register their identities on different platforms and numerous websites. They are then required to create, remember, and use different passwords. It is not possible to update all these databases at the same time. Another huge risk posed by current identity management systems is that a hacker just needs a single break on a single major database to gain access to numerous identity records. Not only does this compromise users' identity but exposes them to potential fraud and loss of money. It is clear from this information that current data identity systems and structures are not business friendly and unsustainable. Fortunately, the blockchain offers a reasonable solution.

Blockchain Digital Identity Solutions

Blockchains provide for the storage of personal data in immutable, trusted, and decentralized records. The technology used ensures that your identity is kept in an incorruptible and secure manner. You will always be able to update your identity with new information in the future should the need arise.

Today, there are numerous companies rushing to develop solutions, powered by the blockchain, for digital identity authentification and management. Some of the companies working on blockchain based identity management solutions include Cambridge Blockchain LLC, Existence ID, Bit Nation, and Civic, among a few others. Some of these companies seek to provide identity services similar to governments.

Companies such as Civic focus on protection from identity theft and prevention of fraud. Take the example of Cambridge Blockchain, LLC. This firm is engaging with financial institutions such as banks in order to create user-friendly and intuitive digital identity management solutions. Their aim is to provide a solution that fully complies with national privacy laws and regulations. The solutions being developed need to be robust if they are to attract major firms.

We also have developments by Secure Key Technologies and IBM. Together, these two firms are creating a digital identity platform with a network of consumers. It will be based on blockchain technology and will be based on a Hyper Ledger Fabric. A Hyper Ledger Fabric is simply a blockchain that has set permissions or a blockchain where users restrict membership. Users of this upcoming digital identity platform will have the capacity to assign permissions regarding those that can access their digital identity information.

Government Identity

There are governments that are already implementing blockchain-based solutions. Governments of India and Estonia are currently working with centralized digital identification programs. What can such an identity be used for? You can use such an identity to access banking services, vote in local or national elections, register property, file tax returns, access other government services, and so much more.

One challenge that governments face is that since they collect the data, it is their responsibility to ensure that it is secure. Such data, when stored at a centralized location, poses a risk, especially as it creates one single point of failure. Therefore, very high-security levels will be required in order to keep the data secure, safe, and away from hackers and identity thieves. Centralized data storage is tantamount to compromise and hence the need for blockchain based solutions that do not have a single point of failure.

Consumers need to be really convinced by the blockchain identity management firms of the benefits of such systems. This is because many have had bad experienced with data breaches, hacking, identity theft incidents in a similar manner. They are therefore pretty hesitant to just join any platform demanding their personal details. Also, the industries that look to adopt this kind of technology include healthcare services, banking, and credit card companies.

Insights from Blockchain Identity Startup

Daniel is the founder of a blockchain startup in Switzerland. His company has come up with a blockchain identity solution that has borrowed from Estonia government's blockchain combined with trust and strong values from his country. His aim is to create an excellent e-government service platform. His team had viewed first hand the application of e-voting technology where participants on the government system were able to vote using their mobile phones. There are a couple of things that stood out after a workshop for developers.

1. There is a need for digital identities to be augmented with individual credit scores. Applications running on the blockchain can be designed to feature details like social media profiles, history of loans repayments, personal income, and so on. Such information can play a key role in easing the process of investing in property, buying a home, and even selling property. In such a situation, a smart contract with all the right details will run on the platform and will self-execute with all the relevant information.

Potential financiers will have access to interested property buyers, their details, and a smart contract that provides the framework for an agreement. If a financier loves a profile and is willing to finance their property, then full disclosure can be made at this stage and the transaction will proceed.

2. When it comes to matters of online shopping, then we can use some concept known as KYC or Know Your Customer. This helps to demonstrate a consumer's trustworthiness. KYC is a reputation management system that supports and enriches general information on a consumer. It provides businesses with both qualitative and quantitative insights about their customers. With this information, they can then come up with different products for their customers.

3. Digital identity also comes in handy in the food chain. This is because nowadays the safety and origins of food cannot be guaranteed or verified by a middleman. Only participants in a given chain can do so with some authority. In order to find out more about a certain food item, all you will need as a business owner or consumer is a simple barcode. This barcode, when scanned, will reveal information that is crucial to the safety and well being of the particular foodstuff. The barcode will reveal verifiable information pertaining to a particular product.

These few examples just go to show how drastically the blockchain is going to affect our lives in the coming days. As a business owner, it is wise to examine these applications, solutions, and even challenges then find which solution would best meet your needs.

Blockchain provides secure and trusted digital identities that will enable businesses and consumers to transact and interact with confidence. It is possible that in less than five years, we will all have a digital identity online with all our private information stored there. It will make it very convenient to achieve certain things like online shopping and accessing government services.

It will also be great to know that such information is very secure, away from prying eyes and is impossible to hack or compromise. Only with such guarantees will the next generation identity systems work to our satisfaction and be universally acceptable. The most popular blockchain solutions are probably the ones that will achieve both leverage network effects and a critical mass of users.

For Business Owners

If you are a business owner, then you need a database and a digital identity system that has integrity, is trusted by consumers, and is incorruptible. We have heard the news about major firms having their databases hacked by cybercriminals. Credit card details, passwords, and other personal details have been stolen the sold over the internet or used for dubious purposes.

Thankfully, the blockchain solution has brought an end to these challenges. With records that cannot be altered or compromised, you can feel safe engaging with customers and taking and storing their personal information. There are blockchain applications out there that will help you manage your business professionally and ensure that your data and files are safe and incorruptible.

Find a firm that has developed and implements global standards when it comes to digital identity management. A decentralized, digital, point-to-point exchange of information enabled by the blockchain is the best solution that you need. Such a system allows for improved privacy, compliance with regulations, ability to update data entries, increase trust, and reduce interaction time. These are some of the properties that you will notice with a blockchain-based system.

Chapter 6: Blockchain and Supply Chain Management

Managing a supply chain is never easy even when you are running a small business. It involves a complex web of trucks and warehouses and an interconnectivity that is full of inefficiencies. These inefficiencies tend to increase costs and this cost is often passed on to consumers.

There are currently some technologies in use within the supply chain management. These include the use of machine learning, artificial intelligence, fulfillment centers and similar technologies are currently being used to help ease the complexity of supply chain and make it more efficient. However, there is another type of technology that holds the promise of changing the game completely.

This is the blockchain technology. Blockchain is currently being developed to help manage different sectors of the economy including banking, the stock market, digital identity and so much more. The supply chain is no different and stands to benefit immensely from this new technology. In all areas where it is finding application, blockchain is causing a revolution. It is speeding up processes, providing superior security, and has helped reduce costs significantly.

The supply chain is one sector that could benefit immensely from blockchain technology. The blockchain could provide suitable solutions for challenges such as product traceability, supplier payments, and even on bidding and executing contracts. If properly applied, blockchain has the capacity to become the global standard for managing the supply chain system. It not only increases security but helps with scalability and improves transparency.

Challenges of Modern Day Supply Chains

Today's supply chain processes are totally complex. A lot of them have no transparency as they lack interoperability. They also operate without consistent data which is sometimes altogether unavailable.

There is a reason why these supply chains are growing more and more complex. Consumers around the world are generally demanding the most innovative products at an affordable price and delivered in a timely manner. Such demands are creating enormous challenges for logistics companies and the entire supply chain. It is a challenge to create a supply chain that is both responsive and cost-effective. Here are some of the challenges inherent in this sector.

1. Globalization

Most firms in the logistics and supply chain sector face a huge challenge trying to cut back their costs. Many companies are going to extreme measures such as relocating to areas or countries where the cost of manufacturing is significantly low. The aim is often to cut costs, minimize taxes, and offer products or services that are more affordable. This is because customers today demand affordable products that are delivered on time.

2. Customer Service

It is important to provide quality customer service to customers especially when they encounter challenges. The supply chain process is all about providing customers, regardless of their location, with quality products, in the right quality, and in a timely fashion. This may sound simple enough but it is quite a complex feat to achieve.

3. Market Growth

Supply chain firms also experience challenges as they pursue new customers. Getting a product from research and development to the market is a costly affair. Companies often endeavor to expand distribution especially to emerging markets around the world in order to grow revenue as well as gain market share. Companies are expected to increase their market shares at home while expanding into larger markets overseas. These pose additional challenges due to prevailing government policies, fees charged and even trading policies that are in place.

4. Customer Preferences

As things are, the process of getting a product to the market from the production line is a complex one. Even then, customers often demand newer and better products all the time. A new product could be released this year and within no time customers are demanding the next big thing or an improvement of the current one. This introduces a new layer of pressure on companies to up their games, get back to the drawing board and think of ways to satisfy customer demands.

Customer demands and expectations are getting significantly higher as time goes by. Companies respond to these demands by creating global networks, expanding markets, and increased product design and innovation. This is the reason why companies are increasingly relying on the supply chain management to ensure that they remain competitive. This is why managers in this field are in such high demand. This is also why there is increased focus on better ways of providing solutions that will provide efficiency at lower costs and faster turn-around times.

Additional Factors Affecting the Supply Chain

There are other factors that also come into play that make the supply chain quite challenging. Think about something like cost-control. Many firms are really putting pressure on management to cut back on operating costs in order to remain competitive. Unfortunately, the cost of energy and rising freight costs, increased labor costs and so much more are all affecting the supply chain and this makes it a challenge to the firms and managers.

To stay competitive and remain both effective and efficient, companies are often assessing, reassessing, and redesigning their strategies all the time. These adjustments, while necessary, are often in response to a frequently changing global market. Any risks within the system need to be identified and sorted out as soon as possible.

Also crucial are relationships between suppliers and partners. It is crucial that a positive atmosphere is created that enables excellent working relations. Experts recommend having a single system that is compiled with as this will ensure there are cordial relations between supplier and business partners.

Introducing the Blockchain to Supply Chain Management

We have already established that managing a supply chain is not an easy feat. In fact, companies are employing specialists to provide recommendations on how to make the systems faster, cheaper, and more efficient.

Fortunately, there is now blockchain technology. This new technology promises to greatly improve this area of specification. Many describe the blockchain as a decentralized ledger that cannot be hacked. It is also described as a record-keeping mechanism that makes it safer and easier for businesses to interact and cooperate over the internet. This can be crucial when it comes to the supply chain process.

Blockchain was initially designed for financial transactions. However, it is a superbly flexible technology that can be customized to handle many different types of problems. When it comes to matters pertaining to the supply chain, the blockchain could make it easy for businesses to track all essential metrics such as location, quantity, type, color, amount, time, and so on.

Basically, blockchain will see the development of a system that allows businesses to get a much better view of what is happening within the entire chain. The blockchain makes it a lot easier for managers and business owners to track compliance efforts as each step is recorded on the network. It is expected to save businesses lots of time. The global shipping industry is expected to save billions of dollars annually with the successful implementation of such a system. Currently, the giant computer firm IBM is working with Maersk, the world's largest shipping firm to develop a suitable blockchain

How the Blockchain Network applies to Supply Chain Management

As an incorruptible ledger, the blockchain has the capacity to store data relating to all products within a chain. A well-designed network is capable of accurately recording each time a product switches hands and indicating each time a product is stored or sold. It will also include so much more data such as arrival time, quantities involved and so on, making the work of supply chain managers, supervisors, and workers so much easier.

Blockchain will make supplier chain management more efficient

Business owners will be able to track a product, using the blockchain, from production to packaging, shipping, warehousing, and display, until the point of purchase. There are numerous advantages when a company is able to have a system accomplish all these.

With this kind of accurate information, experts and analysts will be able to inspect the system and identify any flaws, inefficiencies, human errors, and delays. They will then be able to design a more efficient system that is less prone to human errors and void of deficiencies. It will also enable a business and its various departments to work closely together in order to achieve the same ambitions.

Blockchain will also enable the supply chain management work better in different aspects. For instance, a business will improve the recording and data entry, tracking of purchase orders and receipts, and all essential paperwork. Other crucial data such as what type of fresh produce is in transit or if a package is fragile and should be handled with care and so on. Here is a closer look at some of the benefits of using blockchain technology is supply chain management.

Benefits of Blockchain

Among the top benefits of incorporating blockchain solution in the supply chain management is the accurate collection of data and how it can be used by multiple departments within the chain to coordinate matters and make the process more efficient. Companies and businesses using this technology are easily able to share data with everyone along the supply chain from manufacturers to transporters, other suppliers, warehouses, and vendors.

This kind of transparency is crucial as it helps reduce delays and improve efficiency. It prevents disputes, reduces delays, and also protects shipments from getting lost or pilfered. It is not possible to lose packages when they are tracked and monitored in real time.

Blockchains are scalable and offer virtually unlimited databases. These databases can be accessed from anywhere in the world through connected nodes. There is also a much higher level of security that ensures all data, files, and relevant information is secure and cannot be compromised. Blockchain can also be customized as required in order to take care of needs that might be specific to a particular industry. Also, the logins are given only to those with express authority to log into the system. It is almost impossible for unauthorized persons to access the database.

The most valuable aspect of the blockchain solution is that it brings together all the crucial data pertaining to a particular operation. When there is one bank of information available to all players, it becomes much easier to manage the operation, coordinate all aspects and reduce inefficiencies within the system. It also helps prevent any form of fraud because information entered into the system cannot be altered or compromised in any way. According to a logistics expert from North America, the immutable records provided through blockchain increase trust in the system and results in smoother operations.

Supply Chain Transparency

The latest blockchain technology has introduced new levels of transparency in the field of supply chain management. According to experts, this new technology improves transparency and also ensures there is traceability of all activities and a reduction in administrative costs.

For Businesses

As a business owner, you want to be able to have accurate and verifiable records of all transactions regarding the logistics, shipping, warehousing, and sale of your products. Blockchain supply chain solutions will help all participants along the chain to accurately record dates, the price of goods, certifications, quality, and all other crucial information. It is the availability of this information in real-time that makes it possible to trace products within the supply chain, avoid gray markets, lower losses, improves compliance, and visibility and so much more.

Chapter 7: Networking and Internet of Things

Yet another great application of the blockchain is in the field of networks and networking. Blockchain, also known as a distributed ledger, has been successfully used in the field of cryptocurrencies. The internet has been amazingly successful and provided connectivity to hundreds of millions of people across the world.

Blockchain is expected to be an added layer on top of the internet. This could help to ease the costs and tedious work of tracking and managing huge networks but without the need for a centralized database. Such a network would not be limited to the Internet of Things or IoT but is versatile enough to find numerous applications.

When it comes to the Internet of Things, we will be able to communicate remotely with devices and gadgets remotely via the internet. Devices will also be able to communicate with each other and perform certain functions without any human intervention.

The Internet of Things

We have already seen that the Internet of Things or IoT is the technology of the future. This kind of technology enables us to control devices remotely and also allows devices to communicate with each other.

The most important aspect regarding the Internet of Things is the network. Currently, IoT operates uses a centralized database and server to manage devices. There are numerous ways that your business can utilize this technology and benefit immensely from it. Think about cooling and heating your storage facilities, turning on security sensors, remote monitoring and so much more.

For the necessary trust to function within an IoT system, there needs to be a powerful network. Current centralized systems have been compromised before and this has affected trust and proper functioning. During attacks on centralized systems, IoT devices cannot act as required because the system does not deem them sufficiently smart without the aid of a centralized database.

On the blockchain, data is distributed across the network and this makes it almost impossible for unauthorized access. Data is therefore stored across numerous nodes and made instantly accessible to all users. In IoT networks, however, it is much better to use a private blockchain network than a public one.

One of the main concerns that people have, including business owners, is the security of their installations and networks. A lot of experts believe that blockchain is the only platform that provides the necessary network needed for the successful launch of IoT. This is because blockchain brings scalability into the equation, will decentralize trust and security from a single point of weakness and onto a variety of nodes within the network.

According to experts, blockchain technology does not just improve compliance and ensure high levels of security. It also introduces cost efficiency as well as useful IoT features. Smart contracts also come in handy because they are able and well placed to monitor and oversee IoT processes. The smart contracts are usually executed when certain set and agreed conditions are met.

There are a couple of ways that IoT can take advantage of blockchain technology. One of these is trust building. By using blockchain, users are able to build the trust needed to ensure devices and gadgets are working as required. There is also the aspect of cost reduction. With its reliability, speed, and effectiveness, it is easy to bring down costs as layers of workers and others are eliminated from the equation.

Blockchain introduces speedy data exchanges because, by its very nature, it is a superfast network. Data can be transmitted from nodes to the devices and other components of the IoT. There is scaled security, which is very important. A lot of the concerns raised by business owners, companies, and institutions such as universities include the issue of security. A security breach can cause a lot of damage to a brand.

It is evident that blockchain technology provides the suitable infrastructure that is necessary for two devices to interact directly and accomplish a set task. For instance, it is possible to place an order through a mobile phone such as turning on a car alarm, regulating the temperature within a building, and things of that nature.

Another important aspect of the blockchain is its capacity to act as a medium of transferring assets. It is possible to transfer an asset such as land or property via the blockchain. This makes it a crucial and even integral part of the financial services sector. This is probably why blockchain based architecture is becoming the standard for most business applications. The traditional data center with a single server and centralized data storage is fast being replaced.

For seamless and rapid transfer of data, edge devices which play a bigger role in bandwidth speeds and networking are absolutely crucial. As such, data center equipment and infrastructure need to adapt to this new approach.

Blockchain technology is able to assimilate a cooperative and distributed cloud storage platform over a peer-to-peer network a reality. This approach makes it possible to increase operational speeds while lowering expenses and charges. Security is hardly a concern in these kinds of setups because of use of cryptography technology. This technology that uses mathematical formula and principles of computer science makes it almost impossible for anyone to decipher data or penetrate the nodes.

Such technologies are in use in many places around the world. Businesses are taking advantage of these new opportunities to take a lead in the market and stay ahead of the game. Even then, there is still plenty of ongoing research and development in different aspects of blockchain technology. It is absolutely imperative that business owners remain focused on developments in the field of blockchain technology.

Blockchain Technology is the Future

Blockchain technology is said to be the most disruptive technology since the advent of the internet in the 1980s. It is going to affect all kinds of industries and not just those mentioned in this book. You can expect to experience it in an industry that you are closely associated with in the near future.

Most experts think it is inevitable that we will eventually have to switch to it. As business owners and managers, it has inherent benefits as has been displayed above. Not only does it streamline operations but makes it harder for unauthorized persons to breach systems and compromise data. The benefits of this new system will definitely and ultimately outweigh all other current systems.

Experts believe that those who adopt this new technology early enough will stand to benefit the most. It is up to business owners to remain abreast of developments within their relevant industries and take advantage of any new developments whether it is new software, networks, and similar technologies. It is also a great idea to start educating yourself early enough about the blockchain, its features and why it is considered in such high esteem.

Conclusion

Thank you for making it through to the end of this book, let's hope it was informative and able to provide you with all of the tools you need to achieve your goals whatever they may be.

The next step is to see where you can apply the knowledge gathered through reading this book. The technology described here, blockchain technology, is the latest cutting-edge technology that is causing ripples in different industries and sectors of the economy. A lot of tech experts think that blockchain is the most significant development in the digital world since the advent of the network.

The next revolution will, therefore, be a digital revolution. Technologies such as the Internet of Things, use of Smart Contracts, distributed ledgers and so on are definitely exciting and will replace the current digital technology. This will mark the fourth industrial revolution which is the digital revolution.

Finally, if you found this book useful in any way, a review on Amazon is always appreciated!

www.ingramcontent.com/pod-product-compliance
Lightning Source LLC
Chambersburg PA
CBHW071244220526
45468CB00002B/993